HOMETOWN FOLKS

Kenneth Pobo

Copyright© 2023 Kenneth Pobo
ISBN: 978-93-95224-66-6

First Edition: 2023
Rs. 200/-

Cyberwit.net
HIG 45 Kaushambi Kunj, Kalindipuram
Allahabad - 211011 (U.P.) India
http://www.cyberwit.net
Tel: +(91) 9415091004
E-mail: info@cyberwit.net

Printed at VCORE.

Thanks to the editors of these journals for publishing work from this collection:

"Under Our Eaves" Interim

"Griefbites" Two Thirds North (Sweden)

"Mary At Thirty" Gnarled Oak

"Mary At Sixty" Gnarled Oak

"Joseph And Fartherhood" Hawaii Pacific Review

"Story Of A Divorce" Parhelion Literary Magazine

"Edwina And The Family Album" Parhelion Literary Magazine

"Ash Forgets" In Parenthesis

"Mrs. Panterluck Says" Ink, Sweat & Tears (England)

"Sunday Slap" Public Republic

"Orchids For Chase" Fine Flu

"I Knew This Guy" Occupoetry

"Jennifer's Pet Peeve" Lost Coast Review

"Jennifer Among Zebras" Adirondack Review

"Rosalee Howe" Northwind Review

"I Bought Johnny Rivers' *Slim Slo Slider* There" Belfield Literary Review (Ireland)

"Aunt Katy Sits" 2River View

"L'il Red" The Five-Two

"Gym Gents" Breakfast All Day (England)

"Trina After The Divorce" Windward Review

"Frank After The Divorce" Windward Review

"Vicki At Twenty" Spokes (England)

"Vicki's Matches" Comrades

"Annette" Ken*Again

"It's Us" A New Ulster (Northern Ireland)

"Over And Out" Tipton Poetry Journal

"Standing Around In A Cemetery" Atomic

Contents

UNDER OUR EAVES

Time broke a branch
against us: summer

nights, ripe berries
I'd eat unwashed, moonjuice
on my shirt. Goldenrod
and fireflies, neighbors
talking beside our garage,
each trellised bean,
an edible saint.
Thirty years ago.

Now when I visit,
we stay indoors.
With a gaudy laugh
a neighbor rattles
trash can lids,
taps on windows, rakes
in heavy rain,

her house falling
apart. Ours, neat
as a geometric proof.

Summer brings chill.

A squirrel eats
a sunflower
by the rainpipe:

stalk bent over,
toothy seeds.

I fall asleep, dream
of trash can cymbals
banging under our eaves.

GRIEFBITES

My dad, 88, tells me he attended
an online funeral on Wednesday,
a cousin's wife, "a fine person
in every way." Grief pulled an

electronic curtain apart so he
could sit with the others
3000 miles away. The wake began
at 1:00pm EST,
before his ping pong game
in the retirement center rec room.
He finished his ice cream
while scrolling through
remembrances, one of which
he wrote. No funeral parlor smell,
no sound of too-tight shoes
walking up to the family
and expressing sorrow. A click

closed the curtain, the screen
dark. Mourning slipped
between keyboard keys.

MARY AT 30 THINKS ABOUT 60

Maybe Elton will give me grandchildren,
cute as ten-cent Cokes. I'll take them uptown
where the purple martin houses decay,
the diner where I met Joseph's gramps
now a gun shop.

I won't wear make-up,
not even lipstick.
If I'm called a frump,
so what? We're all frumps
after a certain age, men too.

I'll ride my bike to garage sales,
buy cookbooks and trellises,
take a train trip across country,
New York to Seattle, have an affair
somewhere around Omaha,
nothing life-changing.

Don't ask about Death.
I'll cling to life like a dahlia
tied to a flagpole. Unless
I'm sick. Morphine and bed sores.
Mom died at 62. It came fast,
like a stone dropping from a bridge.

60 seems far away. A twig
dropping into the bird bath.

MARY AT 60 REMEMBERS 30

When I turned 30
my friends dumped me at a table
in a dark bar, ordered me a daiquiri.
I sat silently as they remembered
the old days—less than fifteen years ago.

When I got home, I broke
the bathroom mirror,
gathered the shards,
and watched a *Flying Nun* rerun.
Sister Bertrille would be cute
forever. Joseph already preferred
PBS science specials to kissing.
Or did he? I thought he did,
accused him of infidelity
which wasn't true—

then. Today I think about 30
and get the glooms. Memory
has old scores to settle,
selects flavors that it craves,

leaves the rest. I may make it to 90.
What will 60 feel like then?
The years varoom. I'm walking
against traffic, no one slowing down.

JOSEPH ON FARTHERHOOD

Sometimes I'd like my family
to enter a spaceship headed to Europa.
The farther away they are,
the more I relax. It's not that

I don't love them. I do.
They're like lugging a hill
on my back week in and week out.
Kids stir a cauldron
of credit card debt and toss me in,
a daddy stew.

I don't tell Mary this. She says
I'm distant, a tennis ball rolling
into a river and floating out of sight.
I'm a good dad. I don't miss
Elton's baseball games,
don't scold him if he strikes out,
which he does more than the others.
If Edwina wants ballet lessons, I pay
and watch her practice. If only

I could be alone, even a few times
a month. Stand outside at night
and look for Saturn,
my family near the rings, me
driving a fast snowmobile
on Earth, waving without stopping.

STORY OF A DIVORCE

Mary and Joseph are, according to their college friends,
a great fit. Ask them to name
their favorite fruit and together they say "Plums!"

They get married at St. Broadbander's on a June afternoon.
Mothers cry. Fathers pat fathers on the back.
Children die beside rivers.
They begin their eager lives. Jobs come
but drop like cell phone signals.
Mary has a tough pregnancy, a boy named Elton East.
Mary has an easy pregnancy, a girl named Edwina.
Elton throws silverware at visitors,
Edwina stabs her pillow with a fork.

Mary decides marriage is a nosebleed. Joseph decides
marriage is a Ford with a flat. Just like that.

Now they live on opposite sides of town,
sharing custody. "50 is the new 40,"
grins a TV star stirring a pot of paella.
Crack an egg for breakfast and you've lost another day.

Mary is alone. Joseph is alone.
Text messages miss their recipients,
run like mice under blushing red maple leaves.

EDWINA AND THE FAMILY ALBUM

Before their divorce, Dad stayed
for a month in the Holiday Inn
where a lunch cook bled
into the potato salad. Lies
slept in the same bed

as truth. Tonight I'm deep
in a family album—in one picture,
mom's buried in a book,
Vonnegut? She looks
like she'd crossbow the camera.
Dad rarely smiles in pictures.
I'm like him. His parents stayed
together, happily and sadly.
Pictures make them look like goldfish,
one inside the glass castle,
the other out.
Mom's parents had the perfect
marriage, I guess. Maybe so,
though perfect aches in quiet.
Do I need

to get married? It might be
like high school. All you want
is to get somewhere else.

ASH FORGETS

I may fall in love. Like finding a ruby
on a shark's tongue. I might find God,
a black hole with sparklers.

In a week I'll be 36.

An old guy at the gym told me
"After 50, it all goes." Ash forgets
the fire that made it. Then
blows away.

MRS. PANTERLUCK SAYS SHE DOESN'T KNOW

why she keeps dis-
appearing. One minute she's
in a mall walking over
to a perfume kiosk and the next
she's gone. It's like she misplaces

her skin. Wherever she is,
she retains a brain, though
Mr. Panterluck often refers to her
as brainless while watching
his fifth game show of the day.

It's strange to be disembodied,
hard enough getting someone
to help even when fully visible.
Still, it does make you better friends
with wind, also invisible,
but powerful too. Mrs. Panterluck

sees herself as a stoplight—
on, off,
on again. Three colors
that keep disappearing.

SUNDAY SLAP

My Sunday School teacher mom
wears a green dress. In baggy pants,
bow tie, I'm picturing Mama Cass,
Question Mark and the Mysterians,

Keith. Glenn laughs, talks out
of turn, interrupts. His mom, Lydia,
stalks in, gives him a SLAP
across the face. Glenn,

no expression, like he wants
to cry but not when a guy's started
junior high. Mom looks away,
tells us of Peter who got out

of the boat and walked on water
since Jesus said he wouldn't drown.
The room's capsized.
Saltwater fills our lungs.

ORCHIDS FOR CHASE

Chase is like an orchid,
offering color, pleasure,
a brightness when winter aches.
She coaxes much into blossom:
a family, friends, students.
We grow under her
patient touch.

When the lights fail and we fear
we'll stumble down the stairs,
Chase is a candle,
a kind word telling us
that we'll be fine.
The storm clears.

And there's Chase, tending to
a bud, readying the room
for a bloom.

I KNEW THIS GUY

who for many years had
a lot of money
a nice home
a nice family
that he complained about but
paid every bill until

he lost his job
just like that
no warning

his stocks blew up
debts mounted

the house moved away
from him
courtesy of the bank

he often said he hated
kooks and creeps
who rabble-roused and
protested
hoped the cops
would round them all up
and imprison them

He changed

Courageously

he faces

pepper spray and weapons.

JENNIFER'S PET PEEVE

Invite long-winded, talky people to dinner. Serve gasoline and
light them on fire. Gather around with marshmallows on forks
and roast them.

Even when the long-winded talk, talk, talk, their words are
skunks letting loose, each syllable a dark alley a mugger leaps
from to get your money.

I know a long-winded man who can't stop talking, ever. This
jukebox with only one song informs us of this over and over.
Being near him is like driving into a tunnel at night—his words,
bats smashing against the windshield.

The long-winded secretly yearn for quiet. This is the one heaven
they will never enter.

JENNIFER AMONG ZEBRAS

In Kenya she expects
magnificent scenery,
finds it, gets bored,
tours protected lands,

sees a lion and black
low-flying vultures, hears
wind gnaw thin trees.
Turn back, she says,

but the driver speeds up,
passes five zebras,
not like those she's seen
in a zoo—these break

into a run, no fences
or gates, stripes—
black paint
on passing clouds.

ROSALEE HOWE

Pimply sophomores hated her,
not because she was mean—
they just despised Latin. Every

few years some Virgil lover
would appear. Rosalee,
the happiest piece of chalk, until

she returned to a cold tundra
of indifference, steeling herself
before her classroom. Colleagues knew

little about her, heads bowed
while grading. After retiring
she gave her beloved texts

to Good Will, a tax deduction.
Few visited. A year later she died.
Principal Abbot renamed the school library

in her honor. Kids texted behind
the dictionary's large bunion.
English teachers cramped

at computer desks—when no one
was looking, some wrote
loveletters on empty screens.

I BOUGHT JOHNNY RIVERS' *SLIM SLO SLIDER* ALBUM THERE

The head shop, Kite Bongs,
sold pot paraphernalia near
the paper products factory.
Sometimes I'd go there
after painting my church
clothes crazy colors,
cut the pants into shorts—

Kite Bongs closed decades ago,
gone like plastic pink flamingos
that flew from primped yards
and never returned.

AUNT KATY SITS

Aunt Katy
or Catherine as she prefers
but nobody calls her that
sulks in the big gold

chair while Aunt Ruth
chatters about her days
with Warren who left her
for his secretary but
years before they lived
in style in Highland Park

Katy won't smile
politely
having lived
on a Wisconsin farm
with a man
who preferred his mother

she has only
the gold
chair's arm
and a silence
that could set
a fire.

LIL' REDD

He goes to the rugby field
and draws swastikas, Stars of David
and the ever-popular "Suck D*c."

As a gay man I wonder about
the "Suck D*c." The bad spelling
advertises his fantasy
he writes out large in public—
a coming out
while he thinks he's staying in.
Naturally, accompanied by pictures
of guy genitals. Maybe

if he spells it wrong, the truth
slips away. Instead, it turns
the field into his own gay bar,
private in public, says who
he really is, wearing the latest
swastika, a popular design now.
Lil' Redd, like Little Red Riding Hood
who entered a stomach
to await rescue. Come out,
Lil' Redd, there's work to be done.

GYM GENTS

In the whirlpool
elderly gents say
it's terrible how
states now can't pass
laws against *fags*.
One says: *It's*
all sex, all they want
is sex. The others nod.

In the whirlpool too,
their territory. Yeah,
I want sex,
like sex, don't see
that as a problem. Don't
they want sex?

I'd also like to lounge
in a whirlpool unpoisoned,
would like to talk about
dahlias spinning bright
petaldiscs:

I am a
homowhois
sexualwho
wantslove,

also someone who botches
up gardens, starts over,
digs needs of seeds.

TRINA AFTER THE DIVORCE

We watched an *I Love Lucy*
where Ricky ends the show
by spanking her. Frank laughed
and laughed. I left the room,
decided we should divorce.

He never spanked me,
though his words hit pretty hard
and often. 23 years,
how many times would I anger him
over the angle of the wreathe
on the door? A just-so husband,
everything done as demanded.

Before we married I liked how the sky
never stopped changing,
never stopped moving. Along the way
I stayed indoors more and more,
a thirsty houseplant. I thought:
it would be a relief

if he died. He hardly contested
my decision. I walked out of the Court,
saw how dark the sky had turned,
a storm sky, maybe dangerous
and welcome.

FRANK AFTER THE DIVORCE

During our last months I lounged
in the basement, filled a coffee can
with nickels, ate peanutbutter crackers
until I felt sick. Trina and I said little.

Perhaps I should never have married.
Our parents wanted us to—
or we'd be living in sin. Actually,
we lived in sin for most of it,
sins of omission, sins of staring
at screens or TVs until we barely
recognized each other. Had she
asked "Are you happy?' I'd have lied.
I should've asked her. What if
too much truth overflowed the banks
of our marriage? Our kids
knew something was wrong—
we were a family of drive,

eat something. Funny,
clearing my coats out of the closet stung.
I thought of spring, how yellow irises
by the garage would bloom as always—
and quickly disappear.

VICKI AT TWENTY

I want to blow torch
each house, axe each mail
box. We live
for cars, sports, clothing—
nothing tidies up nothing.

Body snatchers, they want me,
can only live if another dies.
I'm a spy, undercover
but visible. I'm nothing

if not dramatic. My parents
think like the rest do—
I should live according to
their grief. I stay quiet.

Oh, to get lost,
lost for good,
nothing in my way but me.

VICKI'S MATCHES

Matches, statues with blazing

heads. I take a whole box
behind the garage,
light one after another.
Fire pulses toward my fingers.
Mom calls me a firebug, says
I'll come to no good,
her favorite holiday,
July 4th, the sky a million
matches blooming.

Will she come to no good too?

ANNETTE

With each day she takes
care of her mother, a volcano
grows in her bedroom. Mother

hangs on hard, demands
a total sacrifice, which she gives,
angry at waking
to a volcano she tries
to hose down, pull up,
shovel out, but smoke
stinks, thickens.

When mother dies, lava seeps
onto the floor, burns
huge holes. Her secret.

She locks each door even
to walk to the store,
draws blinds. Unbearable heat.

A terrible rumbling.

IT'S US

We dunk Earth
in a carbon boil,
temperatures off the charts,
seas rising. When I die,
Norfolk may be gone.
At church Father said
we must have hope.
An ambulance speeds by.
Where is it going?
Our house? Can't be.
Yes, it's us. And
it's too late.

OVER AND OUT

Three cop cars pull up to their home—
Janet lies on the front lawn.
They take her away alone.

Buried under drugs, her cell phone
used for making deals, supply gone.
Three cop cars pull up to their home.

I hear her groan,
my porchlight off, blinds half drawn.
They take her away alone

to the police station's white bone
walls, her face wan.
Three cop cars pull up to their home

to nab her from her family's own
fury—the house silent till dawn.
They take her away alone

as if she's stone,
this frightened fawn.
Three cop cars pull up to their home—
they take her away alone.

STANDING AROUND AT THE CEMETERY

You stare at the spot
where your dad lies,

I stare at two deer
eating flowers left
to honor the dead—
still hungry,
they bound off
to back yards
and lilies just about
ready to bloom.

www.ingramcontent.com/pod-product-compliance
Lightning Source LLC
Chambersburg PA
CBHW020853160726
47993CB00004B/1643